CAUSES AND CONSEQUENCES

OF THE

VIETNAM WAR

CAUSES AND CONSEQUENCES

CAUSES AND CONSEQUENCES

OF THE

VIETNAM WAR

DAVID WRIGHT

RSVP
RAINTREE
STECK-VAUGHN
PUBLISHERS
The Steck-Vaughn Company

Austin, Texas

Published by Raintree Steck-Vaughn Publishers,
an imprint of Steck-Vaughn Company

Developed by the Creative Publishing Company
Editor: Deirdre McCarthy-Morrogh
Designed by Ian Winton

Raintree Steck-Vaughn Publishers staff
Project Manager: Joyce Spicer
Editor: Shirley Shalit
Electronic Production: Scott Melcer

Cover photo (large): American helicopters airlift supplies
Cover photo (small): Viet Minh flags in Hanoi, 1954

Library of Congress Cataloging-in-Publication Data

Wright, David K.
   Vietnam war / David Wright.
      p.   cm. – (Causes and consequences)
   Includes bibliographical references and index.
   Summary: Discusses the causes of the Vietnam War and traces its course from the early stages before American involvement to the 1974 ceasefire and its aftermath.
   ISBN 0-8172-4053-5
   1. Vietnamese Conflict, 1961-1975 — Juvenile literature.
[1. Vietnamese Conflict, 1961-1975.]   I. Title.   II. Series.
DS557.6.W75   1995
959.704'3–dc20   95-17256
                                                         CIP   AC

Printed in Hong Kong
Bound in the United States
1 2 3 4 5 6 7 8 9 0 LB 99 98 97 96 95

CONTENTS

WHAT WAS THE VIETNAM WAR?

Explaining the Vietnam War is like using chopsticks to pursue the last grain of rice in a complex Asian dish. The object is no sooner grasped than it slides away, easily seen yet difficult to hold.

The war as we know it began about 1960 with the introduction of American troops into Vietnam. It ended in 1975 with the capture by Communist Vietnamese of the southern capital of Saigon. In those fifteen years,

The Vietnam War brought over a decade of horror to the small Southeast Asian country and a political headache to three successive U.S. administrations. In this picture, American helicopters airlift supplies into a landing zone at Khe Sanh in South Vietnam.

millions of lives were lost or deeply affected and billions of dollars spent. Equally important, the world teetered on the edge of an even more serious conflict throughout that turbulent period. Whether a "brushfire war," a war of liberation, or a stand against communism, the Vietnam War could easily have escalated into world war or into a world-ending duel between two or more nations armed with nuclear weapons.

Those involved in the Vietnam War may disagree on when it began or when it ended. They certainly differ as to its causes and consequences. To a Vietnamese raised in northern Vietnam, the war may be seen as a fight for independence, against various foreign foes, spread over many centuries. To some southern Vietnamese, the conflict started after a decision made half a world away to split the country in two in the 1950s. Other southern Vietnamese, Communists who fought beside northern forces against the southern government, see it as a grassroots revolt.

Vietnam's next-door neighbors, the Chinese, the Kampucheans (formerly Cambodians), and the Laotians, were also affected by the war. Both Laos and Cambodia were invaded by U.S. soldiers pursuing Communist Vietnamese and suffered heavy bombing raids. China, having supported the Communist Vietnamese during the war, later invaded Vietnam briefly "to teach the Vietnamese a lesson" after Vietnamese troops stormed into Kampuchea to overthrow the Khmer Rouge (Communist Cambodian) government that had been responsible for millions of Kampuchean deaths.

REAPING THE WAR'S PROFITS

In contrast to the carnage and the loss experienced by Vietnam and its immediate neighbors, some countries nearby may actually look back on the Vietnam War as beneficial. It has been argued that the war gave Thailand, Malaysia, Singapore, and other countries in Southeast Asia the time to prosper and strengthen — to prop themselves up against internal and external foes. The war certainly made many people wealthy. In contrast, many Australians, Filipinos, Koreans, and Thais gave their lives honoring political commitments made by their leaders over Vietnam.

The war meant something different to the citizens of two countries that had strong links with Vietnam —

South Vietnamese civilians flee from a village near Saigon during an accidental napalm bombing raid by their own air force in 1972. The French introduced jellied-gasoline bombs, known as napalm, during their war against Vietnamese Communists following World War II and it continued to be used by Vietnamese and American pilots. Such incidents helped turn Vietnamese peasants against the government, while images of civilian suffering published by the Western media did much to fuel anti-war sentiment around the world.

France and the Soviet Union. The French were finally defeated by the Vietnamese in 1954 after trying to keep Vietnam a French colony. For a French citizen, the loss of Vietnam marks the twilight of a once-mighty empire. The Soviets were aware that their country gave away millions in arms and aid for years to the Communist Vietnamese when the money could have been better spent at home. Neither France nor the Soviet Union learned from their experiences in Vietnam — the French were forced to depart Algeria in 1962 and the Soviets fought a war much like Vietnam in Afghanistan throughout the 1980s.

Other countries remember the intense feelings caused by the war. In Germany and Great Britain, firm U.S. allies, governments either backed United States involvement or remained silent. In contrast, German and British citizens in huge numbers protested against the war. Canada and Sweden became places of refuge for peace-seeking American soldiers and for U.S. civilians avoiding military service. In Cuba and Central America, Communists who regarded the U.S. as a conservative bully took heart at seeing it being humiliated by a small impoverished nation. Citizens of developing nations and members of uprooted populations in the Middle East studied the hit-and-run tactics of the Communist Vietnamese and immediately began to practice their own brand of guerrilla warfare.

AMERICANS VIEW THE WAR

Within the United States the memory of the war is still a painful one and provokes many contradictory opinions. Among those with the strongest views are:

• America's 8.2 million Vietnam-era veterans. Most who served in Vietnam put the war behind them and got on with their lives. But for some, the war will never end. They dress in combat clothing, they fail to find or keep work, they are obsessed with their personal role in the war, and they mourn the loss of more than 58,000 American lives. They wonder if the 153,000 disabled ex-servicemen are being treated fairly by the federal Veterans Administration. Many believe there are American prisoners of war still held captive somewhere in Indochina.

• Antiwar activists. As the war dragged on, larger numbers of ordinary citizens protested against the war. These people were joined for the first time in history by people on active military duty and by some veterans. Minorities believed they were used as cannon fodder and were often in the forefront of antiwar protests. In fact, the war was fought largely by the sons of patriotic, working-class Americans, usually the last to abandon a prowar stance. As the peace movement began to attract more Americans of all kinds, President Richard Nixon turned in 1969 to "Vietnamization" — reducing the number of U.S. troops and handing the fighting over to the South Vietnamese.

• Politicians. Congressional leaders consistently found themselves having to catch up with public opinion during the war, becoming increasingly antiwar as the conflict continued. At the war's end, however, the politicians took the lead once again, in one of two ways: They either pledged there would be no more such wars or promised that the next war would be one America would win. The country was more distrustful than ever but preferred the latter argument and became more conservative. Perhaps citizens found it hard to admit that Americans had actually been the "losers" in a war — a war that cost several million civilian and military lives and taxpayers $140 billion. Successful military actions since, in Panama and Iraq, for example, were said to have "put Vietnam behind us."

The misery and divisiveness connected to Vietnam won't entirely be resolved, at least in the United States, until everyone who lived through the war, soldier and civilian, is laid to his or her final rest.

WHO ARE THE VIETNAMESE?

Vietnam is a long spine of mountains with two major river deltas on either end. Its rugged, forested terrain was to prove hazardous to both French and American troops.

The people who call themselves Vietnamese may have been started with a shove. Long before written history the Vietnamese minority were pushed out of southern China by the Chinese, into the fertile, virtually empty, and low-lying Red River Delta in what is now northern Vietnam.

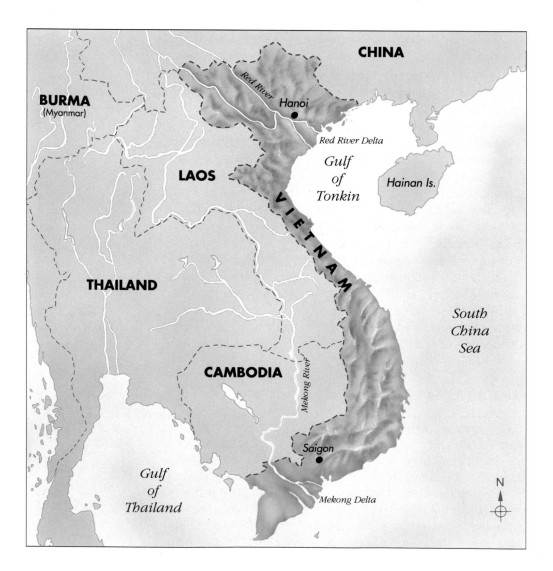

A Buddhist monk prays in a pagoda in Vinh Trang. With its belief in the insignificance of the material world and earthly suffering, Buddhism was attractive to the Vietnamese who were accustomed to hardship and war.

Very slowly, the Vietnamese population grew, expanding to fill the wide valley, one of the earliest sites of wet — or paddy — rice production in Southeast Asia. About 1500 B.C., sailors from what is present-day Indonesia beached their boats on Vietnam's shore and moved as far north as modern China. The Vietnamese mixed with these seafaring people.

China invaded and ruled northern Vietnam for almost 1,000 years, from about 100 B.C. to A.D. 900. Because the Chinese looked on foreigners as barbarians, they treated the Vietnamese as just another inferior tribe. The Vietnamese repeatedly rebelled. Their most successful revolt was led by two sisters, Trung Trac and Trung Nhi, at about the time of Christ. Learning that the Chinese intended to execute her husband, Trung Trac and her sister rallied the people and overthrew dozens of local Chinese rulers. The sisters eventually were defeated by a huge Chinese army and committed suicide by drowning.

THE TEACHINGS OF CONFUCIUS

The 1,000 years of Chinese occupation left indelible marks on the people. Although they grew to despise rule by foreigners, the Vietnamese learned Chinese literature, science, and culture. And while they did not share the same language, they accepted the Chinese philosophy called Confucianism, which honored the past. Combined with Vietnamese ancestor worship,

Confucianism's aim was to use ancient rules in contemporary society. The belief was not a religion. In fact, a disciple of Confucius, who created the philosophy, once said "The Master never spoke of the spirits." Instead, he searched for old guideposts that pointed toward the Tao, or true way life should be lived.

Buddhism was also introduced to Vietnam from China in the second century A.D. It spread from the Red River Valley along the coastline. By the Middle Ages, all of Southeast Asia except Malaysia was Buddhist. The religion seemed to thrive whenever Confucianism was weak; in Vietnam it was particularly popular among the peasants and had an intellectual following among city dwellers and priests.

The Chinese were overthrown and forced out of Vietnam in A.D. 939, but Chinese warlords made later forays into the country. Though the invaders were turned away by valiant citizen-soldiers, the close presence of China was an ongoing source of concern for

This drawing of statues of Confucius and his disciples indicates the importance of the ancient philosopher to the Chinese and Vietnamese. Confucius taught that well-educated people would create a good government, valuing the wisdom of the past while dealing with the present. Confucianism mixed with Buddhism and other beliefs to give the Vietnamese a strong sense of history and duty to ancestors.

Vietnamese rulers and farmers alike. It has been said that "Vietnam and China are as close as lips and teeth." The Vietnamese have lived for centuries in fear of being bitten.

Though the Chinese had departed, Buddhism remained and played a strong part in shaping the country. Education centered around studying ancient texts — the goal was perfect repetition of the past rather than an improved future. The philosophy encouraged people to occupy the same ground as their ancestors and to live as their parents had lived.

As the population grew, the Vietnamese moved slowly south along the western edge of the South China Sea. They mixed with and eventually conquered the Cham people in central Vietnam. The Chams were of Indian descent and had sailed from their homeland to establish a small kingdom, Champa, on the coast of Victnam. By about A.D. 1500, the Vietnamese began to settle far to the south in the Mekong Delta. This fertile area was peopled by Khmers, ancestors of today's Kampucheans. The Vietnamese thus became a blend of many different peoples that also included Thais and various minority tribes living in the thickly forested mountains that run down Vietnam like a backbone.

Traditionally, the Vietnamese majority has clung to the coastline and to the two huge river deltas at either end of the long, narrow country. The hills, highlands, and mountains are thickly forested and thought to hold dangers for lowland people. In fact, the entire country has long been the breeding ground for numerous dread diseases — dysentery, malaria, tuberculosis, and typhoid among them. The waters and wooded areas are home to several species of poisonous snakes, and animals and insects at certain times of the year can be thick and dangerous. Life was simple, potentially dangerous, and often brief.

THE GREAT MONSOONS

The climate of the region has also played a vital role in shaping Vietnamese society. Southern Vietnam has two weather patterns — hot and wet springs and summers and hot and dry autumns and winters. The north is hot and dry each summer and autumn and cool and wet each winter and spring. The climate is caused by monsoons (literally, "huge winds") that move back and forth across southern Asia. One of the reasons for the

A rural scene in Hoa Lu Province, North Vietnam. Rice paddies and limestone outcrops make this one of the most picturesque parts of Southeast Asia. A few rural areas of North Vietnam emerged from the war without being bombed.

reliance on wet-rice production in Vietnam is the fact that there are months with very wet weather, followed by months with no rain at all. Vietnam, said an American soldier, is the only place on earth where you can be up to your waist in water as dust blows in your face!

Because they are modest and because they need protection from the elements, Vietnamese families have for centuries surrounded their small homes and villages with thick vegetation. Looking out across miles of paddies, a visitor notices numerous clumps of gardens, hedges, and trees. Behind each clump of isolated green may live one or more families consisting of two or three generations — mother and father, together with their several children and grandparents. Villages and cities are sites for marketing activity or are located where important roads or canals cross. Before the war in the 1960s and 1970s, the Vietnamese were an overwhelmingly rural population.

Whether farmers or village or city dwellers, the Vietnamese diet is based on rice. It is accompanied by a variety of vegetables, bits of fish, chicken, or pork, pungent sauces, and fresh fruits. Tea and rice wine are popular drinks. Farmers have for centuries grown and lived on rice, eating a large midday meal after four or five hours of field work, then relaxing during the heat of early afternoon before returning to the fields for several more hours of labor.

Vietnamese have traditionally believed that the power of the government — whether foreign or domestic — should end at the village gate. In other words, they did not care what a king or a prime minister or a president might do regionally or nationally, so long as the ruler did not intrude into local life. The average Vietnamese was not highly political, preferring and often forced by circumstances to attend to practical matters of work and family.

This traditional way of life began very slowly to change about A.D. 1500 with the arrival of the first Western settlers, who were Portuguese. These foreigners were looked down on because they did not fit into the Confucian scheme of things. Nevertheless, they posed a problem, for if they were inferior in every way, how could they possess advanced weapons and be able to travel great distances? The Europeans greedily traded coins and trinkets for spices, especially pepper. They established a small settlement near the present-day city of Danang. Hiring themselves out as armed mercenaries (paid soldiers), practicing a strange religion called Roman Catholicism, and treating the local population with contempt, these people were only a hint of what was to come.

So we can see that the nature and long history of the Vietnamese people themselves could be described as a contributory factor to the later, bloody conflicts in Vietnam. Foreign domination, and resistance to that domination had been a feature of Vietnamese life for centuries before the first American troops arrived.

Rice planting takes place in the Mekong Delta. Vietnam is one of the world's major rice-growing areas. Rice paddies stretch for miles across the Mekong Delta in the south and the Red River Delta in the north.

COLONIAL VIETNAM

THE ARRIVAL OF THE FRENCH

French residents and Vietnamese dedicate the first Roman Catholic cathedral in Saigon in 1863. Many hundreds of Vietnamese converted to Catholicism in the eighty years of French rule.

No other country on the Asian mainland was more influenced by Catholicism than Vietnam. The religion was introduced by the Portuguese and spread by French Jesuit priests. These skilled religious teachers first arrived in the late sixteenth and early seventeenth centuries, about the time that the Portuguese empire showed signs of decline. Among the most important Jesuits was a gifted linguist, Alexandre de Rhodes.

Rhodes found a Vietnam very different from the rich, tropical country he had been expecting. Instead it was a complicated place where citizens waded in the rice harvest one year and committed suicide to avoid death by starvation the next. There were complex laws and customs in place, created by the mandarins —

administrators who studied the writings of Confucius. And there was Buddhism, the religion founded in India that developed huge followings in China and Southeast Asia, and in Vietnam was always more popular than Christianity.

Rhodes heard the Vietnamese speak and described the language as sounding like birds twittering. It is a tonal language, one in which a simple word such as "*ma*" can be uttered seven different ways! Rhodes devised a modified Roman alphabet for the language which was easier to teach and to learn than were hundreds of Chinese symbols. It made teaching Catholicism much easier, and gained the religion numerous Vietnamese followers from the seventeenth century onward. But it also created a Buddhism-versus-Christianity environment in a country with a history of warring factions.

For centuries, the Vietnamese had fought among themselves when they weren't rallying against foreigners. By the time of the American Revolution in the 1770s, the country was in the hands of several opposing clans. Also involved in the fighting were French missionaries contributing technology, promising French troops, and advising rulers on the wisest alliances. After decades of strife, a man named Gia Long eventually subdued his enemies and united all of Vietnam in 1802 under the imperial Nguyen dynasty.

In exchange for French assistance during his struggle, Gia Long permitted priests and missionaries to spread Catholicism. Though most Vietnamese continued to be Buddhists influenced by Confucianism, ancestor worship, and even primitive superstitions, thousands turned to Christianity. This was especially true of the people who dealt regularly with the French – they found that Catholicism gained them favor in the eyes of the Europeans. Such Vietnamese were disliked by the country's peasants and by traditional followers of Confucius, who thought they were toadies, hypocrites, and opportunists.

Gia Long's imperial successors, however, felt no obligation to the French and began to punish priests spreading Christianity. Even though Vietnam wasn't the golden land the French had hoped, there were enough French citizens and investments there so that by 1843 a permanent, protective fleet of ships was stationed off the coast of Vietnam. Four years later, French vessels bombarded the harbor of Tourane (modern-day Danang) after learning that a priest had been imprisoned. Tu Duc, the Vietnamese emperor at the time, fully intended to eliminate Christianity—and the French—from Vietnam. However, he underestimated French firepower.

Fighting climate, rugged terrain, and tropical disease, French forces slowly took over Vietnam. They captured the port of Saigon in the south in 1861 and, two years later, conquered all of Cambodia. Throughout the late nineteenth century, the French consolidated their holdings. By 1887 they were in full control of all of Vietnam. The thinly populated, rugged wilderness of Laos was added in 1893. Together, these three areas of Southeast Asia became French Indochina. The region's ethnic groups lost their identity but not their resentment over French rule, which could be harsh.

Rural and urban rebellions began even before the French consolidated their "balcony on the Pacific." A rural, anti-Catholic, and anti-Christian movement soon became anti-French and anti-government as the Vietnamese realized that their emperor had become a mere puppet ruler controlled by the Europeans. The French replaced Vietnamese law with the French penal code in 1886 and began taxing with a vengeance. They taxed everything from opium to salt. Especially unfair was the tax on alcohol, because the French forced each village to accept a certain amount of spirits and then levied taxes on those amounts!

Anti-tax riots broke out across the country in 1908. At least eighteen Vietnamese were executed and dozens more imprisoned before the strife ended. A small minority of Vietnamese with ties to the French continued to do well, while most suffered as France made Vietnam the world's second-leading exporter of rice in the 1930s. The Vietnamese took heart in 1936 when France elected a socialist government. Surely, they believed, the socialists would extend their international tradition of brotherhood to French colonies. Such was not the case, so the Vietnamese

By 1893 the French had taken over the whole of Indochina. Vietnam was divided into Tonkin, Annam, and Cochin-China, while Cambodia and Laos were administered separately.

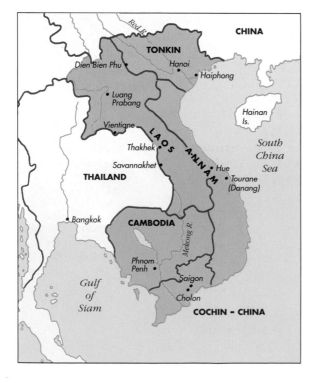

utaged a number of strikes in 1937 and greeted the fall of France to the Germans in 1940 as a blessing.

JAPANESE OCCUPATION

However, it turned out to be something else entirely. The Japanese took control of a huge area in the Pacific beginning late in 1941 with the sneak attack on Pearl Harbor, Hawaii, and the quick capture of Hong Kong, Malaya, and Singapore. The Japanese came to an arrangement with the Fascist Vichy government in France and used French Indochina during World War II as a food source for their troops, while French forces maintained order. Those who profited least from the foreign occupation were the Vietnamese.

The legacy of 450 years of European exploitation and colonial rule must be seen as a cause of later conflict. By the 1940s and 1950s many Vietnamese had simply had enough of foreign domination. An increasing number of natives, especially those in the north, began to look to a different ideology as a path to independence. They placed their faith in a fragile man who had spent much of his life abroad. The ideology was communism and the man was Ho Chi Minh.

Priests at prayer inside the Great Temple of the Cao Dai religious sect. A blend of Eastern and Western religions and philosophies, Cao Dai was also a political force which attracted many followers who wanted independence from the French in the 1920s and 1930s. The sect expanded to one and a half million members after World War II, had its own private army, and became yet another troublesome factor in the complicated politics of Vietnam.

HO CHI MINH

Ho Chi Minh prepares to mount a horse during a military mission against the French in 1945. Ho lived with his Viet Minh forces in rural northern Vietnam during the war against the French, suffering illnesses and narrowly avoiding capture. A lifelong bachelor, he traveled the world as a young man before returning to lead fellow Communists.

Central Vietnam is about 39 miles wide at its narrowest point. Tall mountains and deep valleys run close to the sea, allowing only small stretches of land for rice farming or settlement. Poverty is widespread. Historically, this ruggedly scenic area has produced an unusual number of teachers, religious leaders, intellectuals, and revolutionaries. The most famous native of the region, called the George Washington of his country, was Ho Chi Minh.

Historians aren't sure that the name Ho was given at his birth. He left no diaries or journals, so even his most ardent admirers can only guess at details of his life and his private thoughts. And because he neither married nor remained close to his family, many questions about him are unanswered. This much is known — Ho was born on May 19, 1890, in a small village from which can be seen both the hazy central highlands and the sea. The son of a roving teacher, medicine man, and mystic, he attended local Vietnamese and French schools. He briefly taught before drifting to Saigon and signing on as a sailor aboard a French freighter.

EARLY TRAVELS

After almost three years at sea, Ho earned his living as a gardener in the French port of Le Havre. In 1913 he sailed to the United States on another French vessel. After working as a day laborer and in a restaurant in New York City for a year, Ho then sailed to London and learned pastry-making under a famous chef. By the time he reached Paris after the World War I armistice in 1918, Ho spoke both French and English. He was able eventually to learn Russian and Thai, in addition to several Chinese dialects, aware that such knowledge might aid his country to achieve its independence.

Ho evidently saw the end of World War I as an opportunity. Shortly after President Woodrow Wilson arrived in France to draft the treaty ending the conflict, Ho put together a statement for the Allied leaders. He asked that the colonial peoples, such as the Vietnamese, be given the same freedoms as Europeans. In other words, he wanted the French in Indochina to turn over the government of Vietnam, Cambodia, and Laos to its native citizens. Had the Allies heeded Ho's plea, a future conflict might have been prevented. But the French and British had other ideas.

The future leader of North Vietnam was much influenced by radical thinkers and writers. He attended a political debating society in Paris where Socialists and Communists argued how the world of the 1920s should work. He and many others at the time were impressed that communism had triumphed in Russia in 1917. Eventually Ho joined the French Communist Party in the hope it would provide a way of forcing the French from his country.

In 1924 Ho went to the Soviet Union. He was disappointed that the Communist leaders he met, including Josef Stalin, were more interested in domestic politics than in helping the Vietnamese. But he learned how to organize and he sharpened his writing and speaking skills before moving to China. Living simply, Ho worked as an interpreter while he recruited Vietnamese students in southern China. Arrests and executions of known Communists in 1927 sent Ho scurrying back to the Soviet Union. Showing the patience that would mark his entire life, he stayed for a while in Europe before turning up in Bangkok, Thailand, which had become a center for Vietnamese activists.

Here Ho met the leaders of the three major Vietnamese Communist parties and persuaded them to unite to defeat the French. Under Ho, the factions became one large unit — the Viet Minh. He became the movement's leader, but this did not make life easier. On a visit to Hong Kong, he was imprisoned. Ho persuaded a hospital orderly to declare him dead and he fled into China. Meanwhile, in Vietnam, the worldwide economic depression was making life harder than ever for ordinary people.

THE RETURN HOME

Throughout the 1930s Ho wandered across China and much of Asia and Europe, battling tuberculosis and supporting himself with occasional work on board various ships. During this time there was civil war in China between the Communists, who gave Ho their support, and the nationalist government. The Japanese military took the opportunity to spread its tentacles across China and farther, into Southeast Asia. In the confusion of war, the aging revolutionary disguised himself and slipped into northern Vietnam unnoticed — his first return in thirty years. Ho met his followers in a remote and mountainous cave. He announced to fellow revolutionaries Pham Van Dong, Vo Nguyen Giap, and others that the time for the revolution had come.

Softly spoken and listened to with great respect for the years he had spent as a nomad, Ho told Viet Minh organizers that Vietnamese in all walks of life should take up arms against the Japanese and their French collaborators. He renewed friendships with various Chinese, who were also at war against the invading Japanese. In exchange for aid, Ho promised to fight against Japan any way he could. This promise did not go unnoticed by members of the U.S. Office of Strategic Services (OSS). The OSS, a forerunner of the Central Intelligence Agency (CIA), recruited Ho and his men to rescue Allied flyers shot down over southern China and northern Indochina. Though records are sketchy, one or more downed American pilots were hidden from the Japanese and escorted safely to Allied areas by the Viet Minh during World War II.

The fall of Japan in the summer of 1945 left much of Vietnam unwilling to accept European rule once again. Ho's health had waned, but not his commitment to a united and independent Vietnam. Fighting off dysentery and malaria, Ho was carried by stretcher to Hanoi, northern Vietnam's largest city. Before a crowd estimated at 100,000 people, the 55-year-old man declared Vietnam independent. In his speech Ho adapted some of the great words from the American Declaration of Independence: "We hold the truth that all men are created equal, that they are endowed by their Creator with certain unalienable rights, among them life, liberty and the pursuit of happiness."

Unfortunately, only the Vietnamese themselves, still without power, heeded Ho's speech.

The huge Hanoi rally proved to be important only to the Vietnamese. The Chinese Nationalist Army took advantage of the vacuum left by the Japanese to occupy northern Vietnam briefly, where they ate and stole at will, while British forces maintained order in the south before handing Indochina back to France. As for the French, they were in no mood to give away territory they believed to be theirs. They may have been especially sensitive on this issue, having been so easily defeated by the Germans at home in 1940. Bowing to the Germans and Japanese had cost them prestige among friend and foe alike. Their attitude was reflected in the tough talk of a French general, who sized up the ragtag Viet Minh volunteers and said, "If those fools want a fight, they'll get it."

The rise of a charismatic leader, with a defiant ideology, is a third factor that brought Vietnam into eventual conflict, first with the French and then with the Americans. Ho Chi Minh, his opponents would soon realize, was unwilling to compromise his dream — that of creating a Vietnam united under the red banner of communism.

Vo Nguyen Giap, a law graduate from the University of Hanoi, was chosen by Ho Chi Minh to organize the Viet Minh forces in the early 1940s. He masterminded their military campaigns against the French, the South Vietnamese, and the Americans, all with great success. Giap later became minister of defense for North Vietnam.

THE FRENCH DEPART

DIEN BIEN PHU

French paratroops drop into Dien Bien Phu in a futile attempt to reinforce surrounded comrades in March 1954. The weather worked to the advantage of Viet Minh Communists, who moved men and weapons into the hills seen in the background where there was too much cloud cover for them to be spotted by aircraft.

In the decade that followed the end of the war the Viet Minh under Vo Nguyen Giap tried a number of different tactics against the French. Most failed. They were driven out of the busy northern port of Haiphong and the northern capital of Hanoi. They were chewed to bits on several occasions when they tried to take on the French in conventional battle. They did manage to damage the French by ambushing road convoys and in other guerrilla tactics. Giap finally resorted to luring the French into the isolated area of Dien Bien Phu.

The French, believing they could win a major battle and gain the upper hand in peace talks, went for the bait.

In truth, the French were desperate. In the eight years since their return to Vietnam, more than 75,000 soldiers had been killed — a larger number than the United States would lose when later its turn came to fight. Few of the deaths occurred in major battles. Instead, soldiers were picked off by booby traps, snipers, mortar shells, even tropical disease and infection. Opinion back home in France was almost completely in favor of negotiating an end to the war. The stand by French forces at Dien Bien Phu was an unpopular gamble long before its disastrous outcome. It did not help matters that in Paris governments came and went every few months, which didn't

allow the formation of a coherent policy on Indochina.

It would have been difficult to find a more obscure place to do battle — or a site with so many flaws. Nevertheless, some 13,000 French soldiers set up defenses in the remote mountain valley named Dien Bien Phu in northwestern Vietnam in the spring of 1954. The French, some of whom had jumped into the area as paratroops, were surrounded by a ring of mountains that held 35,000 Viet Minh. Even more daunting, their Vietnamese adversaries had dragged huge artillery pieces into the hills, concealing them in mountain caves and with camouflage. The shells ripped into French forces at will.

There was more bad news. Because cloud cover often hung well below the encircling mountains, French pilots could not see to bomb the dug-in Vietnamese. Nor could they accurately drop supplies to the French, many of whom had parachuted into Dien Bien Phu only lightly supplied and armed. Far from normal lines of supply, the French dug in as artillery fire destroyed everything above ground level. The battlefield appeared as if it had been made to order for the Vietnamese.

The two sides battled throughout the damp spring. France, having convinced the United States that it was fighting communism, went to the U.S. seeking aircraft to attack the enemy. However, President Dwight

French and Vietnamese prisoners of war march away from Dien Bien Phu following the decisive battle that drove the French out of Vietnam in 1954. Communist Viet Minh soldiers surrounded French-led forces, hiding in mountainside caves to avoid French artillery. Gradually, the Communists tightened the circle before overrunning the colonial forces. Few French soldiers survived the long march to prison camp after their surrender.

Eisenhower, noting that his country had spent an estimated $4 billion supplying the French in Indochina, refused to help. Eisenhower had good reason to be wary: the United States and its allies had been fighting Chinese and north Korean Communists on the Korean peninsula for more than three years. Most Americans in and out of government feared land war in Asia and opposed military intervention.

French forces at Dien Bien Phu were too well armed for an all-out assault, so the Viet Minh surrounded them and began to tighten the noose. There were three French artillery batteries and two of them were quickly disabled. Whenever French gunfire became too thick, the Vietnamese dug trenches and tunneled toward and around their foe. Frenchmen who survived Dien Bien Phu tell of hearing the shovels all around them for days on end. The outpost finally was overrun on May 7.

Other than the French themselves, few were sorry to see them leave Indochina. When they arrived, four out of five Vietnamese could read. When they left, only one Vietnamese in five was literate. During the eighteenth century France had become the home of "liberty, equality, fraternity." Yet the French in Indochina suspended rights and laws and manipulated natives with everything from opium and alcohol to bribery. As early as 1945, there were Americans who were opposed to allowing the French back into Vietnam. Though the voices in opposition included President Franklin D. Roosevelt, the French had returned — for eight bloody years. Vietnamese military and civilian deaths in those years reached 300,000, an indication of a real willingness to sacrifice for independence.

A year ago none of us could see victory. There wasn't a prayer. Now we can see it clearly — like light at the end of a tunnel.

French general Henri Navarre, just prior to the battle of Dien Bien Phu, 1954.

THE ROLE OF THE UNITED STATES

Relations between Ho Chi Minh and the U.S. had appeared cordial when World War II ended. But because Southeast Asia was considered less important than Europe, America initially ignored the area. Fearing the strength of the Soviets, the U.S. moved to rebuild a Europe shattered by war. When China fell to communism in 1949, American politicians blamed each other rather than the corrupt nationalist government that had been overthrown. Ho Chi Minh was viewed increasingly by the administration of President Harry S. Truman as a friend of Peking and Moscow and an enemy of Washington. The French weren't ideal allies, but in the 1950s America saw them as the lesser of two evils. Consequently, a large share of aid originally intended for rebuilding postwar France ended up as guns or ammunition in Vietnam.

THE GENEVA TALKS

All Vietnamese — Buddhist, Catholic, Communist, Nationalist — followed the peace talks concerning their country, which took place in 1954 half a world away in Geneva, Switzerland. The Viet Minh now called themselves the Democratic Republic of Vietnam. But they were only one group among many who had interests at Geneva — these also included the non-communist Vietnamese, the French, the Soviets, the Americans, and the British. The talks went on for ten weeks, resulting in a cease-fire and in two agreements. Vietnam was to be divided into Communist North and

Whether the French like it or not, independence is coming to Indochina. Why, therefore, do we tie ourselves to the tail of their battered kite?

Raymond B. Fosdick, U.S. State Department official, 1950.

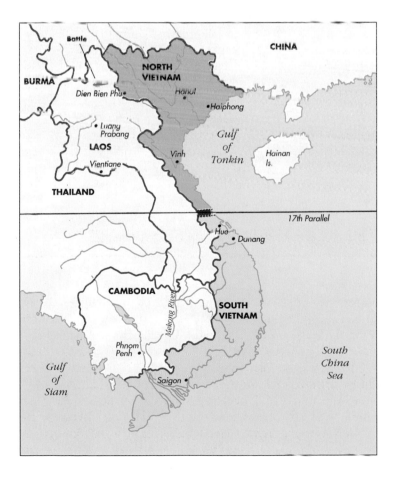

In 1954 Vietnam was divided by international agreement along the 17th parallel into a Communist North and non-communist South. Elections were scheduled for 1956 that would reunite the country, but these were never held.

The flag of the Viet Minh, with a golden star on a red background, was hung all over the city of Hanoi in October 1954 during celebrations to honor the victorious Communist forces.

noncommunist South and there would be a national election in 1956 to determine who should lead the country, which was then to be reunited.

One result of the Geneva agreement took place immediately. One million noncommunist northern Vietnamese crowded onto U.S.-provided boats and planes to flee south, away from government land management and deprivation. A large but unknown number of Communist Vietnamese in turn headed north, fleeing the corruption left as a legacy by the French. Roman Catholic Vietnamese in North Vietnam were among the biggest losers in the wake of Dien Bien Phu. They knew that the Viet Minh was actively anti-Catholic and they watched with apprehension as brutal land reform took place. Frequently, Catholics with more than average holdings were treated drastically, whereas non-Catholics were shown consideration by the new Communist government.

Meanwhile, in the South, the last survivor of the Nguyen dynasty, Bao Dai, who had been the puppet leader of Vietnam under the French, appointed a rigid noncommunist, Ngo Dinh Diem, as his prime minister. A short while later, Diem organized a referendum that threw out Bao Dai, whose enthusiasm for government had always been limited.

Neither side could be proud of the next two years. The North Vietnamese eliminated noncommunist nationalists and the South Vietnamese did the same thing to known Viet Minh who remained in the South. Diem also took on and defeated several well-armed religious sects and the Binh Xuyen, a private criminal gang that had supported the French. He did this clumsily, battling the gangsters in the streets of Saigon, killing 500 civilians and destroying property. Despite the excesses in the North, enthusiasm grew in the South for Ho Chi Minh's government as backing for the Diem government declined.

Behind Ho Chi Minh loomed the Chinese, who worried that American bases would be established in South Vietnam. And behind Ngo Dinh Diem loomed the Americans, who feared that communism would smother Southeast Asia if it weren't halted.

Hardly had the last French soldier left Vietnam before the lines for the future battle were drawn up. Vietnam, like Korea before it, had been divided into a Communist North, bordered to the north by a country (China) determined to defend and export its ideology, and a noncommunist South backed by a fiercely anti-Communist American administration. Confrontation was almost inevitable.

It was vital to compete with Russia in Southeast Asia by encouraging the success of noncommunist political elements in every country of the region.

Robert M. Blum, Drawing the Line, The Origin of the American Containment Policy in Southeast Asia, Norton & Co., New York, 1982.

Ho Chi Minh following the victory over the French in 1954. Few Western reporters had seen Ho prior to his appearance at a truce commission meeting in the village of Thai Nguyen. They learned that the Viet Minh leader had received training in Moscow, but many viewed him as a fighter for independence first and a Communist second.

A TURBULENT DECADE

THE COMMUNIST THREAT

The Reverend Martin Luther King, Jr., waves to the crowd during the March on Washington in 1963. King became convinced that the war was wrong and participated in demonstrations against the administration of President Lyndon Johnson.

Ten years passed between the 1954 Geneva agreement that divided Vietnam and the decision by the United States to fight on South Vietnam's behalf. Americans today might assume their country became suddenly committed to war in Southeast Asia in 1964. On the contrary, Vietnam was an important factor in American foreign policy throughout the preceding decade, and it was political and military decisions made during that time that led America inexorably to war. In 1954 the U.S. regarded itself as the leader of the "free," that is, noncommunist world, and thought that it knew what was best for everyone. Its overriding concern was containing the spread of communism.

Conservative U.S. politicians, led by Republican senator Joseph McCarthy, helped to whip up a state of near hysteria in the country. They accused the State

Department in the early 1950s of losing China to the Communists. They believed there were Americans inside the government who were sympathetic toward communism. To prove otherwise, the Truman and Eisenhower administrations talked tough to the Soviets, to the Chinese, and to other Communist countries. Their policy toward Southeast Asia was dictated by the domino theory, which stated that, if one country in Southeast Asia fell to communism, all would fall, one after the other. Should that happen, Americans envisioned communism throughout South Asia — Burma, India, Pakistan — followed by a Red sweep westward to engulf the entire continent of Africa. The scenario frightened otherwise rational people.

The United States had other reasons besides ideology for aiding South Vietnam. It was aware that Vietnam had immense potential for economic growth. Americans had watched Japan rise from the ashes of World War II and had seen Japanese technology spark enviable productivity in Taiwan, Hong Kong, and Singapore. The former French territory of Indochina was known to have large coal deposits and other mineral resources. Should Vietnam, Cambodia, and Laos — and the rest of Southeast Asia — be allowed to fall into uncooperative hands?

To calm these fears, President John F. Kennedy in 1961 increased the small number of military advisors originally sent to Vietnam by President Eisenhower. Kennedy and his anti-Communist liberals called for more mechanized and mobile armed forces and created specialized troops such as the U.S. Army Green Berets. These elite soldiers were sent into mountainous areas to help the local people improve their situation and to persuade the Southeast Asians to reject communism. Kennedy also took an aggressive stance in other areas of the world threatened by communism. Not all these political or military schemes worked, however. The 1961 Bay of Pigs invasion of Cuba, for example, intended to liberate the island from its Communist leader, Fidel Castro, was a fiasco. However, until Kennedy's assassination in November 1963, America was idealistic and thought much was possible.

Part of this idealism stemmed from the country's hesitant decision to confront discrimination against African Americans. Following a Supreme Court decision in 1954, the federal government resolved that blacks were entitled to full citizenship and equality,

[The] US Must Take Risks in Southeast Asia: Kennedy

Newspaper headline, January 16, 1962.

The creation of a US Military Assistance Command, Vietnam (USMACV) under General Paul D. Harkins on Feb. 9, 1962, marked the opening date of America's direct involvement in the new Indochina War.

Bernard Fall, Street Without Joy, 1964.

U.S. senator Joseph McCarthy testifies about Communist Party operations in the United States in the 1950s. McCarthy believed the country, including the armed forces, was menaced by agents seeking to over-throw democracy. The Wisconsin senator's tactics resulted in his being censured by the Senate, but the fear he aroused played a part in America's decision to fight communism in Vietnam in the fol-lowing decade.

not the so-called "separate but equal" treatment to which they had been subjected. Television coverage of integration created widespread sympathy among many white Americans and added to the small but growing number of social activists in all parts of the country. The struggle for civil rights would soon be overshadowed by the Vietnam War, toward which virtually all activists were opposed.

If Americans had identified correctly the need to address racial problems, they were way off the mark concerning communism. The average citizen in the early 1960s was convinced that the Communist world was more powerful than the West. The U.S. government did nothing to correct this view and for decades was given a blank check by the electorate for the defense of the country. It became almost unpatriotic to point out Communist weaknesses, as this would question the whole basis of U.S. foreign policy. In truth, as it has turned out, the Soviet and Chinese economic, diplomatic, and defense systems were always much weaker than those of the U.S. and Western Europe.

THE VIET CONG

Meanwhile, in South Vietnam, hatred of Diem and his family grew. Among their grievances, people pointed out the corruption of the government, its refusal to share power, and its land reform failures. Viet Minh personnel in the South began calling themselves the National Liberation Front, which appealed to anyone with a complaint against the Diem regime. Diem called his enemies Viet Cong, or Vietnamese Communists. These usually rural people began executing local politicians who supported Diem. The prime minister played into their hands by replacing the dead with military people who did not know or care about the locals. This drove more and more peasants into the arms of the Viet Cong.

By 1963, the situation in South Vietnam had worsened. Outnumbered Viet Cong had beaten well-armed South Vietnamese soldiers of the Army of the Republic of Vietnam (ARVN) in a big battle near the Mekong Delta village of Ap Bac. The enemy invaded Saigon, killing twenty-nine Americans and holding the American embassy for five hours. Two Buddhist monks

A makeshift outfit of about 60 Americans discarded their military advisory role for four hours here Friday to trap communist guerrillas fleeing from the bloody battleground of Ap Bac.

Lead paragraph from story in Stars and Stripes, *January 6, 1963, the U.S. military daily newspaper, which indicated that Americans were participating as well as advising in the fighting*

A Buddhist monk commits suicide on a Saigon street in 1963 to protest against discrimination by the South Vietnamese government. This suicide took place on October 5, and was the sixth such event in South Vietnam that year.

The military events
of this past year in
the Republic of
Vietnam have con-
tributed substantially
both to the develop-
ment of improved
counterinsurgency
techniques and
toward ultimate
victory for the
Republic of Vietnam.

*Report presented to
the Association of
the U.S. Army on
October 23, 1963.*

committed suicide by dousing themselves with gaso-
line and then lighting matches in a protest against
government discrimination toward the Buddhist
majority. Diem's generals agreed that he had to go.
When they revealed a planned coup to the American
ambassador Henry Cabot Lodge, he said nothing to
Diem. The president and his scheming, drug-addicted,
advisor-brother were executed on November 3, 1963.

Throughout this period, American newspapers
were filled with hundreds of reports of bombings and
other incidents in Vietnam that had caused death
and injury to U.S. military and civilians. As early as
1959, two American officers were killed and another
wounded by a bomb while viewing a movie in a Saigon
theater. American civilians, working as engineers,
agricultural advisors, and contractors, went outside
their homes after dark at their peril. By January 1,
1963, more than thirty American military advisors
had been killed aiding the South Vietnamese Army.

Lyndon B. Johnson, who succeeded President
Kennedy following his assassination on November 22,
1963, was told by Secretary of Defense Robert F.
McNamara early in 1964 that the Viet Cong were
making gains. It was known that the guerrillas were
receiving weapons and being organized by the North
Vietnamese and that volunteer soldiers from the North
were moving south along a primitive road hacked
through jungles and around mountains that would
come to be known as the Ho Chi Minh Trail.

More U.S. military advisors and equipment were
sent to prop up the government in South Vietnam but
because the Congress is the only branch of the U.S.
government that can declare war, President Johnson's
options for further action were limited. This limitation disappeared early in August 1964, following the
Gulf of Tonkin incident. U.S. Navy ships, operating on
the fringes of North Vietnamese waters in the Gulf of
Tonkin, reported being fired upon by enemy patrol
boats. Three of the enemy vessels reportedly chased
the USS *Maddox*, which called in aircraft-carrier jets
to fire on the boats. Because navy personnel said they
had been fired upon, the President sought permission
from the Senate to escalate or increase involvement in
Vietnam.

Although the incident occurred in murky weather
and there was some doubt that it had even taken
place, President Johnson received overwhelming support from the Senate after he ordered massive air

strikes along the shores of North Vietnam on August 5, which badly damaged that country's modest navy. On August 7, the House of Representatives voted unanimously and the Senate voted 82-2 to widen the President's options short of an actual declaration of war. This Gulf of Tonkin Resolution, as it was called, came to be viewed by historians as a unique move. It gave President Johnson and future presidents a precedent for making military decisions without the advice and consent of Congress.

During the 1950s and 1960s then, several events combined to propel the U.S. into eventual conflict in Southeast Asia. First, in the wake of the Soviet conquest of Eastern Europe and the fall of China to Communism, the anti-Communist hysteria in the U.S. reached fever pitch. The Korean War had proved inconclusive, and, it was felt, there was a need to make a stand against communism. Secondly, there was growing hatred in South Vietnam for America's ally Ngo Dinh Diem, and growing instability in the country. Thirdly, and allied to the second point, was the growing strength of the Communist Viet Cong in the South.

This map shows the sites of important military engagements during the Vietnam War, together with the Ho Chi Minh Trail. The Ho Chi Minh trail through Cambodia and Laos was used by the Viet Minh to infiltrate men and supplies to the South. Initially it was little more than a series of primitive jungle tracks but it was later developed with roads and bridges to carry heavy equipment.

ESCALATION

THE CAULDRON BUBBLES

The political situation in South Vietnam in the mid-1960s might have been laughable if there had been no war. General Nguyen Khanh, the prime minister of South Vietnam, was no more adept at running the country than the assassinated Diem had been. Buddhists continued to protest, claiming, with some validity, that Catholic politicians discriminated against the Buddhist majority. Their protests delighted the Viet Cong and the North Vietnamese. Khanh was soon replaced as prime minister by a succession of "decrepit characters," as one historian describes them, who had no experience of leading any kind of country, much less a new and troubled land at war.

Not that North Vietnam was running like a well-oiled machine. Ho Chi Minh apologized for his government's land-reform errors. To complicate matters, the U.S. Central Intelligence Agency recruited agents among the Vietnamese who disrupted everyday life in the North, sabotaging factories and blowing up bridges and communication lines. The raids did little permanent damage but were an annoyance. Already a primitive, struggling place to live, North Vietnam became even more deprived as many young men were recruited for military training and sent to fight in the South.

Lyndon Johnson first bombed North Vietnam in August 1964. The raids were soon suspended, but resumed again early in 1965. This picture shows a U.S. Air Force pilot, Robert Shumaker, who was captured by North Vietnamese forces after his plane was shot down on February 11, 1965.

PRISONERS OF WAR

The first American pilot to be captured by North Vietnam was a Californian, Navy Lieutenant Everett Alvarez, Jr. His was one of two planes hit by anti-aircraft fire during the initial, retaliatory raid against the North on August 5, 1964, following the Gulf of Tonkin incident. Like many of the 600 flight personnel who would be captured, Alvarez was injured while ejecting from his plane — he suffered a broken back. The young naval officer was kept in the "Hanoi Hilton," the prisoners' nickname for their Hanoi prison. Somehow, he managed to survive his injuries, lack of medical care, minimal food, and nearly nine years of captivity.

Lyndon Johnson refused to bomb the North again until after the presidential election in November 1964, not wanting to alienate pacifist voters. But beginning on February 7, 1965, and for three years thereafter, North Vietnam was inundated with attacks by planes. To combat the waves of fighters and bombers, the North gladly accepted antiaircraft missiles from the Soviets and the Chinese. With each confirmation that a U.S. plane had been shot down and flight personnel taken captive, the anxiety of American civilians grew. North Vietnam announced that the downed airmen would be treated not as prisoners of war but as war criminals. What did that mean, America wondered. Would these prisoners be executed? It was especially discomforting that no regular line of communication could be established between the prisoners and their families, despite efforts of the Red Cross and religious and pacifist organizations. Scraps of news film from North Vietnam showed prisoners behaving robotically in front of the cameras, often visibly wounded or injured.

The Johnson administration and the North Vietnamese engaged in a war of words. The President said the bombing would stop the moment the North Vietnamese ceased sending fresh troops into the South via the Ho Chi Minh Trail. The North Vietnamese said there could be no negotiation so long as American planes invaded their airspace. While they exchanged words, Americans and Vietnamese were dying with increasing frequency over North Vietnam and on the ground in South Vietnam.

Despite the growing difficulties in Southeast Asia, Lyndon Johnson's first two years as President had

Nothing in the past reaction of North Vietnamese leaders provides any confidence that they can be bombed to the negotiating table.

Robert McNamara, Secretary of Defense, testifying before a U.S. Senate subcommittee, 1967.

I had the weirdest feeling. My airplane was hit and started to fall apart, rolling and burning. I knew I wouldn't live if I stayed with the airplane, so I ejected, and luckily I cleared a cliff.

Lieutenant Everett Alvarez, Jr., recalling years later how his plane was hit .

been almost perfect. Because many in and out of Congress sympathized with the awesome responsibility the Kennedy assassination had thrust upon him, they backed virtually every piece of legislation LBJ conceived. Determined to emerge from the gigantic, legend-fed shadow cast by his predecessor, Johnson proposed far-reaching civil rights measures. He stood firm when southern members of his own Democratic Party abandoned him for his views on racial equality. He even managed to build up the military while cutting taxes and submitting a balanced federal budget — something no President since has been able to do.

An intense, complex man, Johnson's hero was Franklin D. Roosevelt, the American President in the 1930s and '40s who led the country through the Great Depression to victory in World War II with progressive ideas and forward-looking advisors. It was Roosevelt who had spotted Johnson's potential while LBJ was still a young congressman. However, many of the advisors left over from the Kennedy administration looked down on the Texan, considering him a rustic, simple-minded figure.

Like Franklin Roosevelt, who saw his most pressing domestic problems end with the arms buildup for World War II, Lyndon Johnson tried to deal with the nation's domestic problems in a forceful way while he simultaneously conducted an escalating war. It almost worked. LBJ created a social plan he called the Great Society, designed in part to make Americans forget Kennedy's social formula, the New Frontier.

The Great Society would be defined by a vast new civil rights bill, a voting rights act, immigration reform, anti-poverty programs, scholarships for college students, Head Start (a preschool program for underprivileged children), Job Corps (training of school dropouts), Medicare and Medicaid (public payment of health care for senior citizens), the formation of a new Department of Housing and Urban Development to deal with blighted areas of large and small cities, and more. To underwrite all this legislation and the conduct of a war required a great deal of money. The Johnson administration gambled that the war would be a short one and did not raise taxes. The administration also gambled that by committing more troops and resources to the war in Vietnam it could be ended much sooner, allowing the President to concentrate on his plans for the Great Society.

The Great Society has been shot down on the battlefield of Vietnam.

The Rev. Martin Luther King, Jr., 1967.

HAWK VERSUS DOVE

In the summer of 1964 LBJ was preparing for a presidential election in the autumn. He needed Congress to share the possible glory — or the equally possible blame — for committing U.S. troops and planes to battle. He also knew that he would be second-guessed by his opponent in the upcoming presidential election, the Republican Barry Goldwater. Goldwater was a hawk — a militarist — who told potential voters that Johnson was too timid where Vietnam was concerned. Compared to Goldwater, Johnson appeared to be a genuine dove — a person opposed to war.

LBJ's campaign managers played the dove card repeatedly. In a television commercial that since has become famous, they showed a little girl cavorting in a flowery field. The voice-over was taken from a Goldwater speech. Both the visual and the voice were suddenly interrupted by a mushroom-shaped cloud from an atomic bomb. Since China, Vietnam's huge northern neighbor, detonated its first nuclear device only a month before the election, the crude but effective advertisement worked. Johnson was elected in a landslide, winning more than 43 million of 70 million votes cast and taking every state except those in the Deep South and Goldwater's home state, Arizona.

Lyndon B. Johnson became the nation's leader following the death of John F. Kennedy and was elected to a four-year term in 1964. Despite an election promise to keep the nation out of war, America under LBJ became deeply involved in Vietnam. Here he visits U.S. troops at the large naval base at Cam Rahn Bay in 1967. With him in the jeep is General William Westmoreland, senior military commander in Vietnam, who repeatedly called for more troops to be sent to the battle zone.

OPPOSING THE WAR

After World War II millions of American and foreign soldiers were released from the military. They returned to their countries, and started homes and families in record numbers. The children born between 1945 and 1958 in the United States became known as baby boomers. They were part of a huge, postwar bulge in the population that occurred throughout the world.

American baby boomers grew to adulthood at about the same time that the U.S. was becoming mired in Vietnam. The more they saw of the conflict in Vietnam, the less they liked. So they began to protest, and because they were so numerous they could not fail to create a stir.

Protest was already a staple of campus life in the 1960s at the University of California in Berkeley, across the bay from San Francisco. So it was only logical that protests such as the Free Speech Movement and complaints about being in an education factory eventually culminated in protests against the war. Students at eastern colleges such as Harvard University and Brooklyn College were only a step behind their Berkeley counterparts. They, too, joined civil-rights activists and campaigners against the use of nuclear weapons.

I'm against all wars. I did this as a religious act.

Roger LaPorte, 22, member of the Catholic Worker movement, quoted in wire-service story after setting himself on fire in front of the United Nations building, 1965.

CAMPUS TEACH-INS

One especially noteworthy campus protest against the war occurred in the middle of the country at the University of Michigan in March 1965. Some Michigan baby boomers became advocates of radical New Left or peace politics. They joined teachers in skipping classes in favor of speaking out about what they felt was happening in Vietnam. The teach-in concept spread like wildfire from one campus to another. So did New Left politics — in fact, being a radical and being against the war became synonymous. The movement's flame was stoked by the federal government when it decided to increase the number of young men summoned for military service.

The draft was necessary because not enough young men volunteered for the army. Once an American male turned 18 years of age, he was under federal order to register with Selective Service, which provided him with an identification card. Applying for the card made the local draft boards, composed of groups of civilians, aware of available young men.

Not all the ID cards were alike. Full-time high school, technical school, or college students could be classified II-S, or student. That would allow them to complete their education before being drafted. Healthy men not in school and between the ages of 18 and 25 received I-A classification, which meant that they could be taken into the army for two years. The alternative was to enlist in any branch of the military for three or more years. Persons who enlisted were promised special training, while the two-year draftee was promised nothing.

College students began to defy orders to report. Some protested more publicly, attending antiwar rallies where they sometimes burned their draft cards. The first person prosecuted for this offense was David J. Miller, a Catholic pacifist, who burned his card in

Peace demonstrators taunt military police during an antiwar demonstration outside the Pentagon in Washington, D.C., in 1967. Demonstrations grew in size as the war continued and as more and more Americans died in the fighting. At first, demonstrators were young and politically radical. But by 1970, they were joined by adult members of the middle class.

1965 despite the threat of a five-year jail sentence and a $10,000 fine. Dozens of eligible young Americans burned their cards and received various punishments. Despite the spread of antiwar activity from the campus to the streets, polls at the end of 1967 indicated that most Americans still favored LBJ's aggressive moves on behalf of South Vietnam.

The first antiwar teach-in held in the nation's capital took place on May 15, 1965. It attracted a crowd of several thousand. From that time forward, crowds would grow to the point that, by 1970, several hundred thousand filled the streets of Washington in huge collective efforts to stop the war. Each time there was an announcement of additional troops being sent to Vietnam the antiwar movement's energy was renewed. By the end of 1965, 200,000 American soldiers were in Vietnam. That number was 400,000 by December 1966 and reached almost 500,000 by December 1967.

Selective service places a heavy discriminatory burden on minority groups and the poor.

From a Congress of Racial Equality (CORE) statement calling for withdrawal from Vietnam, 1966.

Not all antiwar protestors were college students (nor, indeed, were all young people opposed to the war). The hippie movement, which had sprung to life in San Francisco in the mid-1960s, adopted more radical stances against the war than anything seen or heard at college. Hippie culture, with its rock and roll music, marijuana and other drugs, and casual sex was reflected in the underground or alternative press. These publications, which were frequently amusing if not known for the truth, were widely read and offered a very different perspective on the war and American life. A typical publication ran a headline late in the war that read, "Enemy [meaning the U.S.] Bombs Hanoi."

Other prominent protesters included the Reverend Martin Luther King, Jr., the black civil rights leader, who insisted the war was a racial issue since African Americans and the poor suffered the highest casualties of the war.

By 1970, under the Nixon administration, so many young men were dodging the draft that quotas could not be filled. At the Oakland, California, induction center in May 1969, for example, 2,400 of 4,400 young men ordered to report for the military did not show up. Government figures indicate that, by the end of 1969, a total of 33,960 young men were violating federal law by avoiding military induction. Many of these avoided both military and prison life by going into exile in Canada or other countries.

TROOP MORALE

U.S. troops had no clear idea of their mission in Southeast Asia. They were told to rid the land of aggressors from the North. But this did not match the picture on the ground. Here the enemy seemed to be a family who farmed by day and hid booby traps or served as snipers by night. If these people are our friends, they wondered, why are they treating us like enemies? The antiwar feeling was most noticeable among junior officers, who were also, in many cases, inexperienced. Their lack of commitment and skills put themselves and their units in increased danger.

On the other hand, it was no wonder that the North Vietnamese and the Viet Cong performed well against Army of the Republic of Vietnam (ARVN or South Vietnamese) forces. ARVN troops assumed that the Americans would save them from being overpowered by the enemy. They were sometimes trained by Vietnamese who had paid bribes to keep themselves out of battle. In contrast, there was no one on whom the Communists could depend — Russia, China, and other Communist countries gave arms and supplies but never furnished the North with troops. North Vietnamese and Viet Cong units were kept going by two ideas: to rid their country of foreigners and remove the foreigners' puppet government in Saigon.

A propaganda poster in Hanoi in 1973 protests South Vietnamese military activity and urges the public to defend the country. Such posters helped keep morale high among the North Vietnamese, despite heavy U.S. bombing.

1968

THE TET OFFENSIVE

Hundreds of correspondents from all over the world lived in Saigon so that they could cover the war. Though they wondered about U.S. motives and were skeptical of optimistic reports furnished by the American military, they had little reason to believe things were going badly. After all, President Nguyen Van Thieu had won a national election in 1967 and his prime minister appeared to be in control of South Vietnam's government. So reporters and photographers paid little heed to the large number of fireworks set off in and around the city late on January 30, 1968. The occasion was Tet, the annual lunar new year observance and Vietnam's most important holiday.

Soon, the more experienced among them knew something was amiss. The pop of firecrackers was replaced by the stutter of automatic weapons and the boom of mortars and other explosives. Saigon was under widespread attack! The night sky around nearby Tan Son Nhut air base became illuminated by ghostly parachute flares. South Vietnamese and American forces were engaged in withering firefights. At the U.S. embassy in the center of the city, a blast ripped a hole in the wall surrounding the multistory building. Viet Cong commandos dashed inside, shoot-

A tank provides cover for U.S. Marines in the battle over the city of Hue during the Tet offensive in 1968. Fighting took place for twenty-five days from house to house before American and South Vietnamese forces killed or drove out the last Communist.

ing the military police guards. Though they did not get inside the building, the commando unit held its ground on embassy property for several hours.

Elsewhere, things were equally grim. Cholon, the Chinese section of Saigon, was crisscrossed by waves of bullets as the Viet Cong, and the South Vietnamese and American forces exchanged fire. Bases and cities all over South Vietnam were hit by the Communists. In Hue, which had a reputation for independence, Viet Cong and North Vietnamese troops executed anyone with even a remote connection to the Americans or to the South Vietnamese government. Enemy forces were mopped up or driven off quickly everywhere but Hue. There the battle for control of the city lasted almost a month!

> If you can save a Marine by destroying a house, then I say destroy the house.
>
> *U.S. Marine Corps commander, Hue, Vietnam, February 1968.*

THE CONSEQUENCES OF TET

The enemy was defeated wherever Tet fighting had flared. Yet the impression that remained was that all of South Vietnam was vulnerable and up for grabs and that the Communists had the upper hand. The Tet offensive gave the Americans much food for thought:

- It became evident that the U.S. and the South Vietnamese pacification programs were failures. Once night fell, no place was safe from the enemy.
- The series of attacks had taken friendly forces almost entirely by surprise.
- A majority of Americans in several polls at home favored withdrawing U.S. troops.
- Fighting in rural areas had driven civilians by the thousands into Vietnam's cities. Consequently, crime, prostitution, the black market, and inner-city recruitment by the Communists thrived.
- The Viet Cong suffered huge losses, but between recruiting and continued infiltration from the North, local units soon regained their strength.
- The big losers were innocent civilians, overwhelmed by the powerful weapons being used on both sides. Those unlucky enough to live in "free-fire zones" (areas where there were large Communist concentrations) were considered enemy soldiers by the U.S. and sometimes were shot at or bombed on sight.
- General William Westmoreland, head of American forces, continued to ask for more troops, but more troops apparently did little good and had little or no impact on the guerrillas.

> I thought we were winning the war!
>
> *Reaction of Walter Cronkite, CBS-Television network news presenter on learning of the 1968 Tet offensive in Vietnam.*

A U.S. Army ranger runs for cover during the vicious battle for control of Saigon during the Tet offensive in 1968. The series of attacks by Communist forces surprised many American and South Vietnamese military leaders.

Accordingly, I shall not seek, and I will not accept, the nomination of my party for another term as your President.

President Lyndon B Johnson in a televised speech on March 31, 1968

The pressure on Lyndon Johnson was incredible. Robert McNamara, his secretary of defense, had resigned, and advisors who had been hawkish on the war either changed their views or fell silent. Virtually the only two civilians advocating continued escalation were Dean Rusk, the secretary of state, and Walter Rostow, Johnson's national security advisor. On the evening of March 31, 1968, as cries of "Hey, hey, LBJ, how many boys have you killed today?" rang across the White House lawn, Lyndon Johnson made a nation-wide, televised address. He said he would stop bombing the North, which had not been effective, anyhow, and that he would try to end the controversy by not running for President later that year.

Johnson's decision also was influenced by a series of clashes that had begun in 1967 at remote fire bases near the border with the North with names like Dak To, Con Thien, and Khe Sanh. To interrupt the flow of men and supplies southward, the U.S. military created several artillery fire bases near the Demilitarized Zone, a mis-named line that separated North and South Vietnam. Surrounding the artillery were soldiers, primarily marines, who were in turn surrounded by misty, jungle-clad hills — and enemy soldiers.

Motion-picture cameras, equipped with new and greatly improved color film, recorded these bases being ripped by enemy guns for weeks on end as the young Americans could do little but dig deeper in their fox-holes. The footage, broadcast into American living rooms each evening on network news, was a powerful convincer that lives were being wasted pointlessly. That assumption was reinforced when the bases were eventually liberated by U.S. Army airborne troops while the surrounding enemy simply disappeared.

America's frustration manifested itself in politics. People who wanted to continue the war backed Republican presidential candidate Richard M. Nixon, Democratic candidate Vice President Hubert H. Humphrey, or conservative maverick Governor George Wallace of Alabama. Peace candidates included Senator Robert Kennedy, who was assassinated on the

The place was absolutely denuded . . . like the surface of the moon.

General Rathvon Tompkins, surveying the Khe Sanh area after the siege by North Vietnamese forces, 1968.

An evacuation helicopter follows a smoke flare to a landing spot in the remote A Shau Valley. Fighting in the wilds of Vietnam spilled over into Laos in 1971, with a resounding defeat for the South Vietnamese forces.

Residents of Hue sort through the wreckage of their city following the Tet offensive in 1968. Much of the old imperial capital was destroyed by artillery and rockets, and hundreds of civilians suspected of being pro-government were executed by the Communists.

eve of his victory in the California presidential primary, and Democratic senator Eugene McCarthy, a longtime opponent of Lyndon Johnson's views on the war. The hawks risked being called liars as their claims that the U.S. was winning the war were contradicted by each evening's newsreel footage, while the doves were accused of being too friendly with hippies, Black Power advocates, and welfare scroungers.

Humphrey may have been in the most difficult role of all. He could not, as the Vice President, reject LBJ's war effort. But if he failed to do so, he would appear to a sizeable number of Democrats as too similar to the Republican Nixon. Nixon won in the end as dovish Democrats stayed away from the polls and despite the fact that Governor Wallace earned the support of an impressive 9.9 million voters.

President Nixon's solution to ending the war was Vietnamization — shifting responsibility for defense of South Vietnam from U.S. troops to South Vietnamese forces. The President, however, frequently played both sides against the middle: he authorized the secret bombing of Cambodia to hit the Communist supply line through that country only shortly before reducing the number of American soldiers in Vietnam from

540,000 to 515,000 in mid-1969. All the while, massive antiwar demonstrations, in the nation's capital and elsewhere, continued. They were fueled by events such as took place in the tiny Vietnamese village of My Lai late in 1968.

A number of U.S. Army infantrymen entered the village, and methodically murdered at least 109 and possibly as many as 500 civilians. The incident could not be interpreted as a battle, since those killed were women, children, and the elderly, lined up in a ditch and shot to death. The incident was covered up by officers and enlisted personnel until one man was released from active duty and wrote to his congressman about "something rather dark and bloody" he had seen while a soldier a year earlier. The person in charge of the executioners, Lieutenant William Calley, was arrested in connection with the crime, which had been photographed as it occurred.

Many people, especially World War II veterans, who had served with honor in the army, were stunned. What had happened to their branch of the military? It seemed that the level of violence in this war was vastly higher than in any previous conflict. And much of it was directed at civilians. The hit-and-run guerrilla tactics of the Viet Cong, with their booby traps and sniper fire, had taken a toll on Calley's men. This was their payback, as it was called, though it seemed strange retribution. The incident at My Lai further divided opinion in the United States, which was not appeased by the continued withdrawal and return home of troops throughout 1969.

When Army investigators reached the barren area in November 1969, in connection with the My Lai probe in the United States, they found mass graves at three sites, as well as a ditch full of bodies. It was estimated that between 450 and 500 people — most of them women, children and old men — had been slain and buried there.

Seymour Hersh, My Lai 4, A Report on the Massacre and its Aftermath, *Random House, New York, 1970.*

The man in the dark shirt is a survivor of the My Lai massacre. As many as 500 Vietnamese civilians were killed by U.S. Army soldiers in the tiny village, which was deserted following the tragedy. This mass killing of innocent men, women, and children in March of 1968 was a profound shock to most Americans.

"PEACE WITH HONOR"

As the policy of Vietnamization began to be enforced, hundreds of thousands of Army of the Republic of Vietnam (ARVN) members deserted. They returned to their families, or they led families home that had followed them from training into battle. Many threw off their uniforms and pretended to be Viet Cong who were surrendering to the Chieu Hoi ("Open arms") policy. This plan provided Viet Cong defectors with training and a small amount of money if they laid down their arms and switched sides. Some Vietnamese, who weren't interested in supporting either side, switched several times as conditions changed! It was hardly likely under such conditions that Vietnamization was going to be a success.

Cities such as Saigon, Danang, and Qui Nhon overflowed with rural refugees who would do anything to stay alive. They could earn about 75 cents a day working on an American base, or they could earn even more selling drugs, stealing, or catering to American service personnel with money and, if they were on leave, time on their hands. The strategic hamlet program, devised to make the countryside safe, had been an utter failure. Proof of its collapse could be seen in the large cities, in drainage pipes or cardboard boxes or wooden crates where destitute, displaced South Vietnamese families, without money or skills, tried to live. All the while, Communist forces took control of more of South Vietnam.

As with the Vietnamese military and civilian populations, the morale of the U.S. military deteriorated as the war grew longer. Noncommissioned men were no longer interested in becoming officers. They had heard stories, some true, that the collapse of military discipline was such that young officers were being killed by their own men. Refusing orders, particularly in dangerous, enemy-infested areas, took place more frequently. Other physical signs of the disintegration of authority appeared, too. Peace signs were scrawled

We seek peace with honor.

President Richard M. Nixon, 1969.

everywhere, hair became longer and more unkempt, soldiers were often dazed on drugs or alcohol. Young Americans suspected they were on the losing side of a war that was coming to an end and they did not want to join the casualty list that amounted to 40,000 soldiers killed and 250,000 wounded by the end of 1969.

Another unfortunate side effect of the prolonged war was the breakdown of race relations in the ranks. Blacks had protested earlier that too many frontline soldiers came from minority groups. The Defense Department took steps to ensure that Blacks and Latinos were more evenly spread throughout the military forces, but there were constant feuds between Black Power militants and openly racist whites. Black soldiers developed their own secret signs, salutes, and phrases.

Back in "the world," as soldiers in Vietnam called the United States, an unprecedented number of veterans were joining an antiwar group. Vietnam Veterans Against the War (VVAW) never numbered more than 7,000 men at most, but they were highly visible in their aging, olive-drab uniforms in the middle of marches on the Pentagon or in other antiwar activi-

No Vietnamese ever called me a nigger!

Sign frequently seen among Black participants in U.S. civil rights and antiwar demonstrations.

The city of Quang Tri, capital of South Vietnam's northern provinces, lies in ruins after it was captured by the Communists in May 1972 and held until September. During this time thousands of civilians, government soldiers, and Vietnamese Communists died as the area was pounded by North Vietnamese artillery and American bombers.

Members of Vietnam Veterans Against the War protest in Washington, D.C., in 1971. Though small in number, VVAW gained a great deal of attention. The sight of disabled veterans such as these two men went a long way in swaying public opinion against the conflict.

ties. Among these veterans were some permanently injured ex-soldiers, missing limbs or in wheelchairs, who had come to hate the war. These people gave older, more traditional groups such as the Veterans of Foreign Wars and the American Legion something to reflect on very seriously.

THE WAR AT HOME

In the 1970s the peace movement became more aggressive. "Bring the war home!" urged antiwar activists. They wanted to disrupt the U.S. government, physically ending the war by persuading citizens to refuse military service, by lying in front of troop trains, or even by sabotaging plants where weapons were made. The 10 million poor people in America, given hope a few years earlier by talk of Lyndon Johnson's Great Society, saw a different message in the slogan. Over the years, they had seen more and more government money spent on weapons and less and less go toward helping the poor.

RESPONSES ABROAD

America did have some important allies in Vietnam. Australia played an important part in the conduct of the war, because they shared a fear of Communist expansion. Australia was a member of ANZUS, a post-World War II defense pact that also included New Zealand and the United States. In contrast to most members of ASEAN (Association of Southeast Asian Nations), the Australians aggressively joined the fight against communism in Vietnam. The first troops, a team of jungle warfare specialists, arrived in 1962. Aviators and engineers arrived two years later. All of these troops were sent to Vietnam to train South Vietnamese soldiers and civilians.

As the war escalated the Australians took an active part in ground operations and by 1969 there were nearly 7,700 troops in the country. They were given many unusual — and often frightening — assignments. In 1972 a small number of Australians and several of the 552 New Zealanders sent to Southeast Asia moved into Cambodia to train that country's forces in

The United States has not been in Vietnam for ten years but for one year ten times.

John Paul Vann, retired U.S. Army officer and senior American advisor, 1971.

Funeral services are held outside Hanoi's Bach-Mai Hospital following a bombing raid in 1973. North Vietnam claimed that twenty-eight persons died in an attack by B-52 bombers on the country's largest hospital, which had 940 beds.

Central Hanoi cleans up following a U.S. Air Force bombing raid in 1972. More bombs were dropped on North Vietnam during the war than fell throughout the world during World War II. Yet the Communists continued to funnel men, weapons, and supplies south to do battle.

Merry Christmas Nixon, wish you were here!

Banner unfurled by members of the 1st Air Cavalry Division attending a Bob Hope Christmas Day show in Long Binh, South Vietnam, 1971.

jungle warfare. Both Australia and New Zealand provided an artillery battalion to fight in Vietnam, and Australian infantry personnel saw action from the hills of the Demilitarized Zone to the forbidding mangrove swamps of the Mekong Delta in the south.

Due in part to antiwar sentiment at home, Australians left Vietnam by late 1971, except for a small group of advisors. A total of 386 Australians were killed and 2,193 wounded during the conflict. Approximately 80 New Zealanders lost their lives in battle.

AN AGREEMENT IS REACHED

Henry Kissinger, Nixon's national security advisor and the architect of much of the later conduct of the war, was, throughout 1971 and 1972, holding numerous secret meetings with the North Vietnamese. He and his adversary, Le Duc Tho, agreed late in 1972 on American troop withdrawals, but that agreement was declined by Nguyen Van Thieu, South Vietnam's president. After one last, 11-day round of bombings around Hanoi and the harbor of Haiphong, the two sides renewed talks and reached an agreement on January 23, 1973. "We have finally achieved peace with honor," declared Nixon. The last American soldier departed Vietnam on March 29 of that same year. In January the U.S. ended the military draft, which had stopped being effective several years earlier.

South Vietnam lasted for two years, one month, and one day after the last American soldier departed. For much of that time, Viet Cong and North Vietnamese forces were winning territory from southern soldiers. On April 30, 1975, Communist soldiers rolled unimpeded into Saigon and the war ended. The U.S.-backed government of South Vietnam wasn't the only casualty of the 15-year conflict. American prestige and authority — the right and the power to lead, command, enforce laws, and judge — were also mortally wounded.

Le Duc Tho's profession was revolution, his vocation guerrilla warfare.

Henry Kissinger, writing later of North Vietnam's representative to secret peace talks.

Henry Kissinger and Le Duc Tho greet the press at peace talks in 1973. The two reached a peace agreement after months of negotiations while fighting continued to rage and American troops were slowly pulled out of South Vietnam.

THE AFTERMATH OF VIETNAM

DECEIVING THE PUBLIC

President John F. Kennedy points toward a "difficult and potentially dangerous" spot on the map of Southeast Asia, the small country of Laos. During this news conference, in March 1961, Kennedy warned of Communist rebel operations. Later Kennedy violated Geneva accords by sending thousands more advisors to Vietnam than had been agreed.

The consequences of the war both on the U.S. and Vietnam as well as the other nations of Southeast Asia were many and profound. It was the first war that America had lost, and even worse, it had lost to a poor and ill-equipped third world nation.

The war damaged many Americans' faith in their government and institutions. During the Kennedy and Johnson years, it was felt that strong interventionist government and the new technology of the age could

Ngo Dinh Diem (with cane) tours his summer home near Pleiku in August 1963, accompanied by U.S. military advisor Colonel McCown. Successive U.S. administrations tried to deceive the American people about Diem and his corrupt government.

solve most of the world's and certainly the nation's problems. America owned powerful weapons that would make war obsolete. American technology led the world and the country was well on the way to placing the first men on the Moon. The war in Vietnam shattered these dreams and laid bare the reality. It is not difficult to see why.

American officials misled repeatedly those who elected them and conducted questionable activities in Southeast Asia throughout the Vietnam era. Eisenhower had provided most of the money the French needed to support their war in Vietnam. Once the French departed, the United States created and then propped up the South Vietnam of President Diem. U.S. Presidents distorted information about the corrupt government they had helped to appoint.

President Kennedy authorized secret CIA-directed sabotage against the North, which was in violation of the 1954 Geneva agreement that ended the war with the French. He also violated Geneva accords by sending more military advisors (16,000) to Vietnam than allowed for (658), and it was under his administration that the CIA conducted a futile, decade-long war in Laos designed to prop up a pro-Western prince. Shortly before his own assassination, Kennedy's people secretly encouraged an anti-democratic military coup that resulted in the death of Diem.

DISTORTING THE NEWS

The truth was bent in so many ways that the news media called the daily Saigon news conference by U.S. military personnel "The Five O'Clock Follies." American military leaders became very interested in body counts, hoping that a ratio of, perhaps, 20 Viet Cong dead for each American or South Vietnamese would persuade people that the forces of democracy were winning. They failed to heed earlier warnings by Ho Chi Minh and other North Vietnamese leaders that the North could lose more men, for a longer period of time, than the U.S. or the South Vietnamese could ever imagine.

Another area in which the news briefings distorted truth concerned drug use by U.S. soldiers. Marijuana in particular was almost everywhere. It was as easy to obtain as beer, which was sold by the military for as little as 10 cents a can, and no more expensive. Heroin was available in larger cities by brand name. Since hypodermic needles could be found by anyone interested in looking, it was possible to shoot up cheaply with an extremely dangerous and highly illegal drug. Long Binh Jail (nicknamed Camp LBJ) near Saigon held many desperate, drug-addled American soldiers, but no one was told how many.

DEEP DIVISIONS

The Vietnam War also caused deep divisions in American society. Television had brought the horror of the war right into people's living rooms and many Americans were not proud of what their country was doing. Antiwar activists fought running battles with the forces of law and order, and against those who

If I had been a young lad growing up in Vietnam between 1961 and 1965, I would have been a Viet Cong.

John Paul Vann, former U.S. military advisor in Vietnam, 1971.

called them unpatriotic radicals. Parents quarreled with their children. By the end of the 1960s American society was divided into hostile camps.

In the 1968 presidential election, Republican candidate Richard Nixon promised to "Bring us together." That promise, together with his assurance that he had a secret plan to end the war, was probably instrumental in securing the election of a politican who later was found to have some strange ideas about his power as President.

In fact, Nixon had no secret plan to end the war at all. It was just another election ploy. Other deceptions perpetrated by Nixon and by Henry Kissinger included the cover-up of massive, secret bombings of Vietnamese Communist bases in Cambodia (in violation of federal and international law). From the start, most Nixon advisors knew that Victnamization could not hold back the Communists, but the administration had to implement the policy because U.S. military quotas could no longer be met.

With every revelation of secret fighting in Laos or Cambodia, and with the air war in North Vietnam continuing to rage, the reputation of the United States

American B-52s over North Vietnam. Repeated bombing of the North and illegal operations over Cambodia and Laos won the U.S. administration few friends at home or abroad.

abroad reached an all-time low. Even relations with U.S. allies became cool. Canada had for several years granted a safe haven to young Americans avoiding the draft. France for years denounced the U.S. presence in Vietnam. American ambassadors and other personnel posted abroad were forced to take counter-terrorist measures due in part to the unpopularity of the war in countries such as Italy, Germany, Greece, and Turkey. Meanwhile Communist countries introduced frequent United Nations resolutions condemning the war.

THE PENTAGON PAPERS

In 1971, a secret, 7,000-page report called the Pentagon Papers was distributed by Daniel Ellsberg, a defense expert disillusioned with the war. It contained a collection of confidential analyses and memos regarding American conduct of the war in Vietnam. The Pentagon Papers clearly showed how President Johnson had deceived the American public over early U.S. involvement in Southeast Asia. Ellsberg handed out copies of the document to antiwar congressmen and to the *New York Times*. When the *Times* printed sections from it, Ellsberg was arrested for espionage. Ironically, the judge dismissed the case due to unfair practices by the prosecution — burglars had been paid to break into the office of Ellsberg's psychiatrist. The break-in became part of the Watergate scandal, which eventually forced Nixon to resign.

Daniel Ellsberg, once a prowar advisor in Vietnam, turned against the fighting and in 1971 leaked information showing that the Pentagon had deceived the American people regarding the possibility of early success in Southeast Asia. Ellsberg surrendered to federal authorities in June 1971 in connection with the leak but was found innocent of any charges.

THE "VIETNAM SYNDROME"

During the nearly two decades that followed the end of the war, Americans showed what they thought of their government by allowing Presidents Gerald Ford, Jimmy Carter, and George Bush just a single term in office. Ronald Reagan was elected, then reelected, in part because he suggested that he would have allowed U.S. forces to win in Vietnam.

Defeat in Vietnam contributed to what Jimmy Carter described in July 1979 as the "crisis of confidence" in American society. The "Vietnam Syndrome" kept both Carter and his successor Ronald Reagan from direct and large-scale intervention in foreign conflicts, unless victory was assured. America dared not mount a serious invasion of Iran when student followers of the revolutionary Muslim leader Ayatollah Khomeini seized the American embassy in Tehran, taking 63 Americans hostage; the U.S. did little more than threaten the Soviet Union when that country invaded Afghanistan in December 1979. President Reagan was not allowed by Congress to intervene wholeheartedly to oppose the left-wing Sandinista rebels in Nicaragua, nor the revolutionaries in neighboring El Salvador.

After the Vietnam disaster, successive U.S. administrations were unwilling to involve themselves in military actions overseas unless victory was assured. President Carter and the American people could only watch and pray when Islamic fundamentalists invaded the U.S. embassy in Iran in November 1979 taking scores of embassy staff hostage.

Military service, once considered an honorable duty and expected by most adult American citizens, became an attractive option to unemployment only for the disadvantaged. Part of the problem was the realization that 58,000 Americans had died in Vietnam, 313,616, had been wounded, and nearly 2,500 were missing in action. The families of the latter in particular lost respect for a government that gave them conflicting versions of the status of their husbands, fathers, sons, or brothers. The loss of reputation suffered by the armed forces was finally partially redeemed by their rapid victory over Iraq during Desert Storm in 1991.

Another powerful American institution, the Christian church, came away from the war less able to speak with one voice. On one side were many conservative southern Baptists, Roman Catholics, Christian fundamentalists, and others who saw the Vietnam War as a battle against godless communism. On the other were Quakers, many Roman Catholic clergy, and most mainline Protestant denominations. Father Philip Berrigan, a World War II veteran and a Josephite priest, was one of hundreds of priests and nuns arrested in connection with damage to local draft-board offices. The clergy often disappeared before they could be tried, successfully dodging FBI agents sent to apprehend them.

The thin veneer of respect for leaders has vanished almost entirely. President Bill Clinton, who as a young man opposed the war, was booed by veterans during Memorial Day ceremonies at the Vietnam Memorial in Washington, D.C., in 1993. Hardly any politician can appear before an audience these days without the threat of being heckled.

Regardless of political leanings, the big losers were veterans who, for whatever reason, could not reconnect with society following their time spent in Vietnam. Many vets felt they were shunned by their fellows, ashamed of what their country had done in Vietnam. Rates of alcoholism, divorce, crime, suicide, drug addiction, and unemployment are higher among Vietnam veterans than other sectors of society.

The most deserving are the disabled, who range from men with only scars for memories to those who are in constant pain or confined under full-time care in a federal Veterans Administration hospital facility. As the country tries to address its huge spending deficit, continued care of these veterans, with very real physical or emotional problems, may suffer.

DÉTENTE AND PEACEMAKING

Perhaps the only positive consequence of the Vietnam War was the realization by the United States government that further military confrontation with the forces of communism would be unfruitful. Instead, improved relations between America, the Soviet Union, and China would best serve the interest of both the U.S. and the rest of the world. In this spirit of détente, or easing of tensions, Richard Nixon visited China in February 1972, the first American President to do so. Three months later, the President went to Moscow to meet with Soviet leader Leonid Brezhnev.

These two historic foreign excursions began the process of reversing twenty-five years of Cold War politics, and ultimately led to the very real improvements in superpower relations and arms limitation made during the 1980s and 1990s.

Older and perhaps wiser, Vietnam veterans remember lost fellow soldiers at the Vietnam Memorial in Washington, D.C., in 1986. More than 58,000 names are on the wall, which caused a controversy prior to being unveiled but has since become one of the most visited spots in the nation's capital.

SOUTHEAST ASIA AFTER THE WAR

POSTWAR VIETNAM

Once the war ended, northern and southern Vietnamese found that they did not have much in common. Northerners considered people from the south to be lazy, sly, and corrupt. Southerners felt those from the north were humorless robots, unable to communicate or enjoy themselves. Problems were compounded after northerners took over many of the government positions the southern Viet Cong had coveted.

But there were other, more pressing problems than simply getting along. The country teetered for several years on the brink of starvation. Not all of the farmers displaced by the war returned to their land—many defied authorities in Ho Chi Minh City, as Saigon was now called, by continuing to live as hustlers and street

Jubilant Communist soldiers wave their flag after crashing through the gates of the Presidential Palace in Saigon in 1975. Saigon fell on April 30 as the result of an offensive that began in the winter of 1974-75 and moved south, picking off South Vietnam's major cities, one by one.

people. Also on the street were disabled veterans, a sight as tragic as it was common.

Without money, seed, or fertilizer, the Vietnamese saw their rice crop dwindle. No one gained any weight and many people suffered from severe vitamin deficiencies. Most restaurants in Ho Chi Minh City were closed by the authorities. That was just as well, since food sources simply weren't reliable.

Those who avoided the pain of starvation sometimes were killed or maimed by the thousands of booby traps and unexploded bombs and shells that littered the countryside. Tragedy hit farm families especially hard as they detonated weapons while trying to clear land. Women and children were frequent victims of the bombs, shells, and mines.

The land was no better off than its people. Pollution from various chemicals clotted streams and rivers, as did sewage and fertilizer. Defoliants had been sprayed by U.S. Air Force planes over large areas of rainforest to help locate Viet Cong troops. By war's end these had denuded an area the size of the state of Massachusetts. Numerous tropical diseases began to thrive in the thousands of bomb craters that were often filled with dirty water, and the quantity and quality of preventive

U.S. planes spray defoliant over a jungle that might hide Viet Cong guerrillas in 1965. Over ten years 19 million gallons of herbicides, which killed all vegetation, were sprayed over South Vietnam, leaving large areas of devastation and lasting health problems for the population. Many American GIs also believe they were poisoned by the substances, especially Agent Orange, and that they have passed along the poison to their children.

A Vietnamese man recycles soft-drink cans in Ho Chi Minh City, formerly known as Saigon. The Vietnamese suffered terribly following the war, as the government struggled to meet human needs. Materials for building anything were hard to come by and cans such as these were often used to construct homes or were sold as recyclable material.

medicines disappeared with the last U.S. soldier.

Almost immediately following reunification of Vietnam, large numbers of South Vietnamese were herded into reeducation camps where they were kept as virtual prisoners for months or years. These included many former South Vietnamese officials and military personnel, Buddhist militants, and young activists. The places they were sent to were usually drab, dirty, or soggy. There the prisoners were worked hard clearing land and fed only enough to keep them alive. Clever residents of such camps eagerly devoured the propaganda they were handed so that they could more quickly return to civilian life. There may even have been executions of high-ranking South Vietnamese, though proof is lacking.

Foreign aid disappeared when the United States departed. The Soviet Union to whom the Vietnamese looked for assistance, was unable to fill the gap, so tools, medicine, machinery, and transportation failed to improve. The Vietnamese became dedicated recyclers, turning scraps of metal into saleable commodities. Other countries offered some aid, but the failure of Vietnam to repay a Japanese loan in the early 1980s gave the new nation a sorry reputation.

Vietnam's neighbors, Cambodia and Laos, suffered

equally. In Laos, minorities that had worked with the CIA or the Green Berets were hunted down and slain. Numerous Hmong tribespeople waited till dark in the jungle and swam the wide Mekong River to safety in Thailand. In Cambodia, murderous Khmer Rouge guerrillas took control of the country in 1975, renaming it Kampuchea, and immediately began to kill anyone they suspected of Western or bourgeois (middle class) leanings. One million Kampucheans lost their lives and millions more were sent to virtual slavery in rural work camps. The capital, Phnom Penh, became a barren site of torture and murder.

After several clashes between Kampuchean soldiers and Vietnamese civilians, Vietnam invaded Kampuchea in late 1978. The brutal Kampuchean dictator, Pol Pot, was chased out of Phnom Penh and

Skulls from the Cambodian killing fields are displayed in Phnom Penh. Cambodian Communists, called Khmer Rouge, murdered millions of civilians in an attempt to seal off their country from the rest of the world. Vietnamese forces invaded Cambodia late in 1978, chasing the Khmer Rouge into remote western areas of the country.

These overloaded Vietnamese boats, with a total of 230 refugees, were refused admission to the port of Macau in 1979 and were towed out to sea. Vietnam's boat people often died or were denied shelter after fleeing Vietnam in crowded, unseaworthy vessels. Those who were admitted to refugee camps were sometimes held for years.

forced to live in the jungle. The Vietnamese installed a government under Heng Samrin but they quickly paid for their actions. The Chinese, fearing Vietnamese successes, launched an invasion across their border with Vietnam in 1979. Casualties on both sides were heavy before the Chinese grumpily withdrew after occupying Vietnamese territory for several weeks. Moreover, the new government in Kampuchea was not recognized by China, the United States, or Britain, and the Kampuchean seat in the United Nations continued to be held by the Khmer Rouge.

Following the Hanoi government's repression of the Chinese minority in Vietnam, refugees began to stream out of Indochina in earnest late in 1978. The government, strapped for cash, shamefully charged people who wanted to leave the country large sums. They were then allowed to climb aboard boats that were often unseaworthy. If they survived bobbing aimlessly in the South China Sea, without adequate food, water, or sanitation facilities, and if they weren't raped or murdered by the crew, the refugees ended up in a displaced persons camp.

These camps, run by the governments of Hong Kong or Malaysia or Thailand, soon found their facilities stretched to the limits, while Western countries were slow to admit the refugees as immigrants in enough numbers to ease the problem. After negotiations with the Vietnamese government, which promised not to punish those who returned, Hong Kong began to forcibly repatriate those whom it considered economic rather than political refugees. As the situation in Vietnam has improved in recent years more Vietnamese have returned to their country voluntarily.

A SLOW RECOVERY

During the 1980s the Vietnamese simply had no friends. Not even a steady stream of money and goods from prospering Vietnamese in North America and elsewhere could alleviate the country's suffering. The final straw may have been the breakup of the Soviet Union and the collapse of communism in Eastern Europe. With their own problems, the various countries formerly allied with the Soviets had little aid to give. Consequently, with a highly effective trade embargo backed by the United States, Vietnam was on its own. Though crops gradually improved and trade with other Asian countries increased, the Vietnamese lived poor and simple lives, little better than during the French occupation.

The number of problems caused the government to lose support all over the country. Although most Vietnamese are still rural peasants, the cities became hotbeds of resentment, corruption, and an underground economy that allowed a small number of people to live rather well. The traditions of education, respect for the elderly, and other desirable traits were overwhelmed by the lack of medical care, the poverty of everyday life, and the government's seeming inability to improve.

That situation is now changing. In 1986 the government in Hanoi launched a policy for economic reform known as *doi moi*. Small businesses are flourishing as the official attitude to private enterprise has become more relaxed and free market economics have been introduced. In early 1994 President Bill Clinton bowed to the pressure exerted by the big electronics companies anxious not to lose the opportunity of doing business in Vietnam and lifted the trade embargo with Vietnam. Diplomatic relations are likely to be restored very soon. The Japanese and Taiwanese have traded cautiously with Vietnam and along with Hong Kong, South Korea, and Singapore have invested significantly in the country. Factories have been opened and there is a huge demand for consumer goods, from motor scooters and trucks to sneakers and radios. The government has also relaxed its puritanical views and Ho Chi Minh City throbs once more with commerce and nightlife.

Another bright area is tourism, as Westerners seek unspoiled lands and hospitable people in today's busy, complex world. The country is still largely undeveloped and the Vietnamese remarkably unbitter about the war. Many of the reminders of the war — downed American planes, the tunnels excavated to hide the Viet Cong — are now tourist attractions. The country's many temples, the misty mountains, the silver beaches, and the teeming cities may combine to bring the positive attention to Vietnam that its people deserve.

With tourist dollars, the exploitation of its oil and other natural resources, and a growing economy, the country may soon be able to join fellow Southeast Asian nations in their current economic good fortune.

In modern Ho Chi Minh City, private enterprise is beginning to prosper and foreign goods and investments are increasing rapidly.

CONCLUSION

The tragedy of the Vietnam War was brought about by a number of related factors: a long-repressed people searching for self-rule; a popular and persuasive

leader ready to unlock his people from their colonial shackles; a corrupt government in South Vietnam; a near hysterical fear of communism in the United States brought about by its expansion throughout Eastern Europe and China and the somewhat questionable "domino theory," which predicted that once Vietnam fell, the rest of Southeast Asia would follow.

The result was one of the bloodiest conflicts in history, which left countless thousands dead and many more wounded. Though the South Vietnamese and their U.S. backers officially "lost" the war, there were no clear winners either. Vietnam and its neighbors were left devastated by the conflict. Kampuchea remains locked in instability as the Khmer Rouge guerrillas continue to harass the elected government. The Vietnamese government remained for many years uncompromisingly Communist, with its people among the poorest in the world.

In the United States too, the scars remain. An entire generation was tainted by the bitter memory of the war. Vietnam and its aftermath helped destroy the dream of the Kennedy administration that a just and free global society was attainable. Now, with a President who in his youth was an antiwar protester, perhaps the nation can begin to come to terms with this unfortunate chapter of its past and look forward to a brighter and peaceful future.

After years of isolation Vietnam is now welcoming tourists who are attracted by the country's relatively unspoiled scenery and beaches. China Beach near Danang was once a scene of heavy military activity, but is now a peaceful resort.

GLOSSARY

Agent Orange
A toxic chemical used to kill all vegetation.

ARVN
Army of the Republic of Vietnam. The South Vietnamese army, most of whom were draftees.

Black Power
The ability by African Americans to gain respect through economic and political power.

CIA
Central Intelligence Agency. This intelligence agency gathers information on friend and foe alike for U.S. government use in Washington, D.C. CIA agents were active in Vietnam from 1945–75.

Chieu hoi "Open arms"
This policy was an inducement to get Viet Cong guerrillas to join the side of the South Vietnamese. It involved money, land, and education.

defoliant
In Vietnam, any chemical used to destroy parts of the jungle so the enemy could be seen. Agent Orange is a defoliant.

Democratic Republic of Vietnam
North Vietnam.

dove
An American who opposed U.S. involvement in Vietnam.

grassroots
At the source or basis. Something that is at the basic level.

Green Berets
U.S. Army Special Forces, trained in guerrilla warfare tactics.

guerrillas
Members of an independent unit who take part in irregular warfare, usually harassment or sabotage, against government soldiers or officials.

hawk
An American who favored U.S. involvement in Vietnam.

Ho Chi Minh City
The name given to Saigon after its takeover by Communists in 1975.

Ho Chi Minh Trail
The path from North Vietnam through Laos and into South Vietnam that was taken by North Vietnamese soldiers and supplies.

ideology
A body of concepts that constitute the thinking behind a political or economic system.

Kampuchea
The name given to Cambodia after its takeover by Communists in 1975.

Khmer Rouge
Kampuchean or Cambodian Communists.

linguist
A person who studies languages.

maverick
One who is independent and does not necessarily agree with a particular party or group.

MIA
Missing in action. The term is used to describe soldiers who disappear in battle.

napalm
Jellied fuel packed in bombs and used in flamethrowers. The end product is a sticky, flowing fire.

POW
Prisoner of war. The term is used to describe soldiers who are captured in battle.

radical
Someone who departs considerably from the normal; an extremist.

repatriate
To return or be forced to return to a person's native country.

sabotage
Destruction of roads, bridges, factories, fuel supplies, etc., by enemy agents.

Socialist Republic of Vietnam
The official name of Vietnam following reunification ceremonies on July 2, 1976.

Tet
The annual Chinese and Vietnamese lunar new year, occurring in late January or early February.

Viet Cong
Communist South Vietnamese guerrillas.

Viet Minh
Vietnamese Independence League. A Communist nationalist movement, founded by Ho Chi Minh.

VVAW
Vietnam Veterans Against the War. Unlike most American veterans' organizations, this group was dovish, or opposed to involvement in the war.

Vietnamization
A U.S. policy centered around planned withdrawal of American forces from South Vietnam. The burden of fighting would shift gradually to the South Vietnamese under the plan, which was introduced by the Nixon administration.

TIMELINE

1954 — May 7: French forces at Dien Bien Phu in northern Vietnam are surrounded and, after a seven-week battle, overrun by the Vietnamese. Agreements split the country in two prior to elections that are scheduled but never take place.

1955 — American money and training support a new, anticommunist government in South Vietnam.

1959 — The North Vietnamese begin sending troops, weapons, and supplies down the Ho Chi Minh Trail into South Vietnam. The first American casualties are soldiers sent to Vietnam as advisors. U.S. personnel in South Vietnam total 760 by the end of the year.

1961 — More than 3,200 U.S. military personnel are in South Vietnam by year's end.

1962 — President John F. Kennedy sends 5,000 marines and 50 jets to Thailand to fight communism in Laos. U.S. advisors in Vietnam number 12,000.

1963 — Jan. 2: A small Viet Cong force mauls South Vietnamese soldiers in the battle of Ap Bac.
Buddhist monks demonstrate against the South Vietnamese government. Several commit suicide by fire.
Nov. 1: Ngo Dinh Diem, prime minister of South Vietnam, is overthrown and executed by army officers.

1964 — Aug. 2: North Vietnamese patrol boats attack the *Maddox,* an American destroyer. A similar incident is reported two days later. U.S. planes bomb North Vietnam in retaliation.
Aug. 7: Congress passes the Tonkin Gulf Resolution, giving President Lyndon B. Johnson wide power to act in Southeast Asia.

1965 — Feb. 24: Operation Rolling Thunder begins. This bombing of the North by U.S. planes is in response to Viet Cong acts of terrorism.
March 8: Marines are the first American combat troops in Vietnam.
October: U.S. Army troops defeat North Vietnamese in the Ia Drang Valley in the first major battle of the war. American troop strength reaches 200,000.
Dec. 25: President Johnson halts the bombing, asking the Communists to negotiate.

1966 — Jan. 31: Bombing resumes. U.S. troop strength by the end of the year is 400,000.

1967 — Jan. 28: North Vietnamese say the U.S. must stop the bombing before talks can begin.
August: Secretary of Defense Robert McNamara tells Congress that bombing the North has not worked.
Sept. 3: Nguyen Van Thieu elected president of South Vietnam.
U.S. troops number 500,000 as war protests increase at home.

1968 — Jan. 31: The Tet Offensive begins as North Vietnamese and Viet Cong forces attack South Vietnam's cities and towns. A request for 206,000 additional U.S. troops is made.
March 31: President Johnson announces he will not seek reelection. He orders a bombing halt and asks the North Vietnamese to talk. American troop strength in December is 540,000.

1969 — January: Peace talks in Paris include the U.S., the North Vietnamese, the South Vietnamese, and the Viet Cong.
March 18: Secret U.S. bombing of Cambodia begins.
June 8: President Richard Nixon announces the withdrawal from Vietnam of 25,000 U.S. troops.
Oct. 15: Huge antiwar demonstrations take place in Washington, D.C.
Nov. 16: The story of the massacre of civilians by U.S. troops at My Lai is reported. U.S. troop strength is reduced by about 60,000 soldiers by year's end.

1970 — April 30: President Nixon announces that U.S. and South Vietnamese forces have attacked enemy hiding places inside Cambodia.
May 4: National Guardsmen kill four antiwar protesters at Kent State University in Ohio as protests spread. America has reduced total troops in Vietnam to 280,000 by year's end.

1971 — February: South Vietnamese forces begin an unsuccessful attack on North Vietnamese troops inside Laos.

March 29: Lieutenant William Calley is convicted of the murders of innocent civilians at My Lai.

U.S. troop strength dips to 140,000 by the end of the year.

1972 — May 8: President Nixon announces the mining of North Vietnam's main harbor and intensified bombing.

Oct. 8: There is agreement to end the war between the U.S. and North Vietnam. But South Vietnam's President Thieu opposes the plan.

Dec. 18: U.S. intensifies bombing of North Vietnam.

1973 — Jan. 27: A cease-fire agreement is signed in Paris. The U.S. ends the military draft.

March 29: The last American troops depart Vietnam.

April 1: The North Vietnamese release the last U.S. prisoner of war.

Aug. 14: The U.S. stops bombing Cambodia following a vote in Congress to halt the offensive.

1974 — President Thieu declares in January that the war has begun again.

June: Communists reinforce and resupply their troops during South Vietnam's dry season.

1975 — Jan. 6: Communists capture an entire province, just north of Saigon.

March 15: The South Vietnamese abandon their northern provinces.

April 30: Communist forces take Saigon.

FURTHER READING

Becker, Elizabeth. *America's Vietnam War: A Narrative History.* Clarion Books, 1992

Cole, Wendy M. *Vietnam.* Chelsea House, 1989

Detzer, David. *An Asian Tragedy: America and Vietnam.* Millbrook, 1992

Devaney, John. *Vietnam War.* Watts, 1992

Dudley, William. *Vietnam War: Opposing Viewpoints.* Greenhaven, 1990

Garland, Sherry. *Vietnam: Rebuilding a Nation.* Macmillan, 1990

Hills, Ken. *1960s.* "Take Ten Years" series. Raintree Steck Vaughn, 1993

——— *Vietnam.* Marshall Cavendish, 1991

Hoobler, Dorothy and Hoobler, Thomas. *Vietnam: An Illustrated History.* Knopf, 1990

Kent, Deborah. *Vietnam War: "What Are We Fighting For?"* Enslow, 1994

Kronenwetter, Michael. *The Peace Commandos, Nonviolent Heroes in the Struggle Against War and Injustice.* Macmillan, 1994

Lens, Sidney. *Vietnam: A War on Two Fronts.* Dutton, 1990

Marrin, Albert. *America in Vietnam: The Elephant and the Tiger.* Viking, 1992

Moss, Nathaniel. *Ron Kovic: Antiwar Activist.* Chelsea House, 1994

Twist, Clint. *1970s,* "Take Ten Years" series. Raintree Steck Vaughn, 1994

Wright, David. *Vietnam.* Childrens Press, 1989

INDEX

Numbers in *italics* indicate pictures and maps

ACKNOWLEDGMENTS

The publishers are grateful to the following for permission to reproduce photographs:

Cover (large), Range/Bettmann/UPI
Cover (small), Hulton Deutsch
Range/Bettmann/UPI, pages 6, 8, 23, 25, 29, 30, 32, 33, 39, 41, 43, 47, 49, 52, 53, 54, 55, 56, 57, 59, 60, 61, 63, 64, 68; Sue Ford/ Ecoscene, pages 11, 15, 19, 66; Hulton Deutsch Collection, pages 12, 16, 20, 24, 28; Robert Francis/ Robert Harding, pages 14, 69; Popperfoto pages 36, 44, 46, 48, 65; Robert Harding, pages 51, 67; Tim Hall/Robert Harding, page 70.

Map on page 10 by Julian Baker.